My New York

Majel van der Meulen

Published in 2017 by
Laurence King Publishing Ltd
361–373 City Road
London EC1V 1LR
Tel +44 (0)20 7841 6900
www.laurenceking.com
enquiries@laurenceking.com

Illustration and series © 2017
Majel van der Meulen

Majel van der Meulen has asserted
her right under the Copyright, Designs,
and Patents Act 1988, to be identified
as the Author of this Work.

A catalog record for this book is
available from the British Library.

ISBN 978-1-78067-962-4

Printed in China

Liberty Island

Statue of Liberty

This book belongs to

....

I promise to look, draw, imagine,
color, add, invent, explore, and
make this city mine:
My New York.

Staten Island Ferry

STATUE OF LIBERTY

The Statue of Liberty was a gift of friendship from the people of France. Design your own statues for your friends inspired by their qualities. Are they sporty, funny, creative, curious ...?

STATUE OF ....

FOR: ....

STATUE OF ....

FOR: ....

STATUE OF ....

FOR: ....

STATUE OF ....

FOR: ....

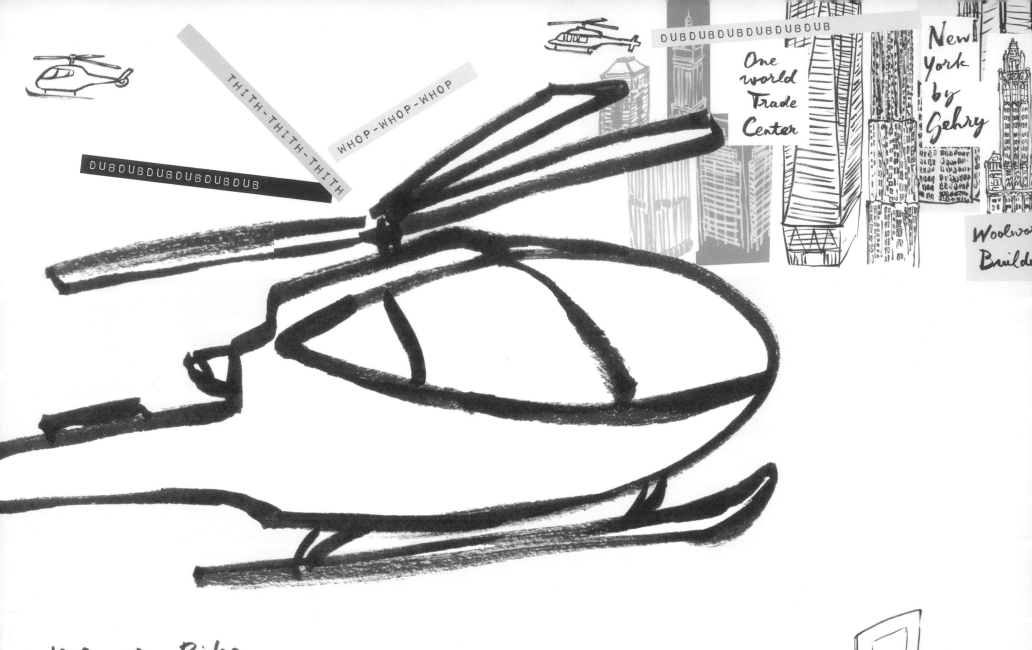

THITH-THITH-THITH

WHOP-WHOP-WHOP

DUBDUBDUBDUBDUBDUB

DUBDUBDUBDUBDUBDUB

One world Trade Center

New York by Gehry

Woolwor Buildi

Helicopter Rides

What's that sound? Look at all the helicopters in the sky!
The police, the air ambulance, and tourists are enjoying a
bird's-eye view. Draw yourself in the cabin!

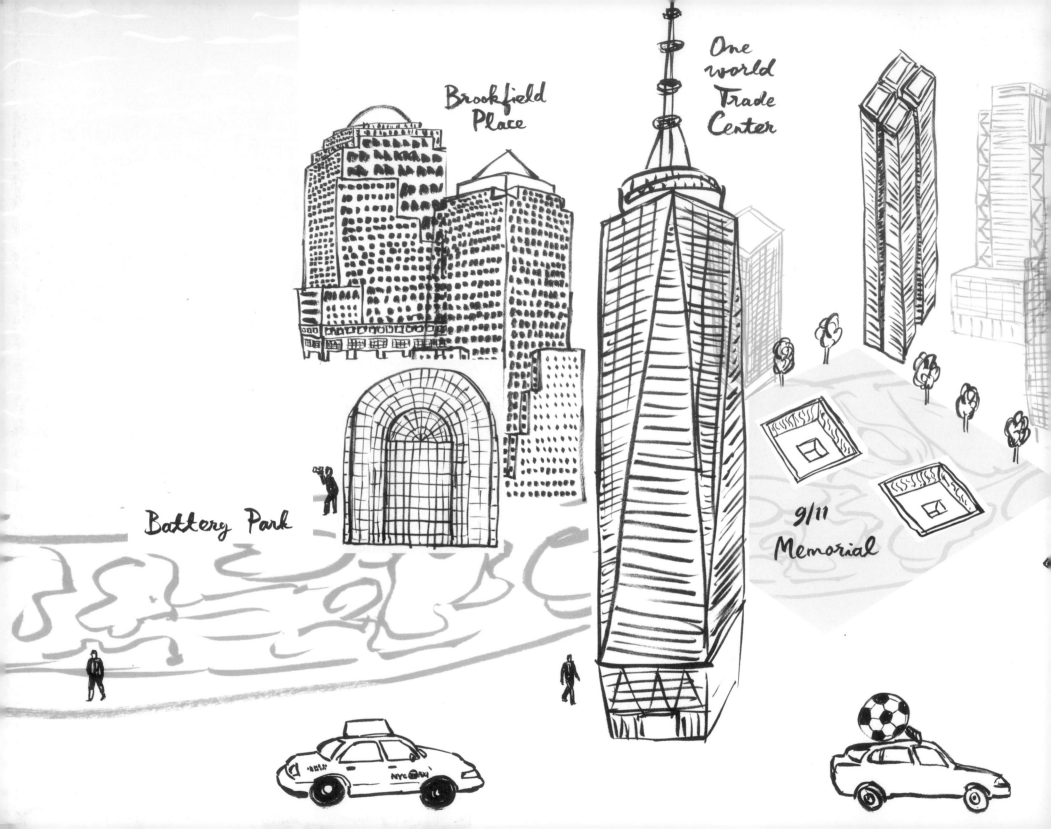

Brookfield
Place

One
world
Trade
Center

Battery Park

9/11
Memorial

NYC TAXI

New York is a whirlwind of activity and iconic buildings, and there's never enough time to see it all. Add some color to the busy streets of New York.

Trinity Church

New York Stock Exchange

Charging Bull

SHOUT IT FROM
THE ROOFTOPS

Besides iconic water towers and
superheroes, there are beehives,
swimming pools, restaurants, and
parties on New York's rooftops.
Draw some events you'd like to
go to on a rooftop!

s Little Italy, so "have a slice", as New Yorkers say!
hoose your favorite toppings and add them to these pizza slices.

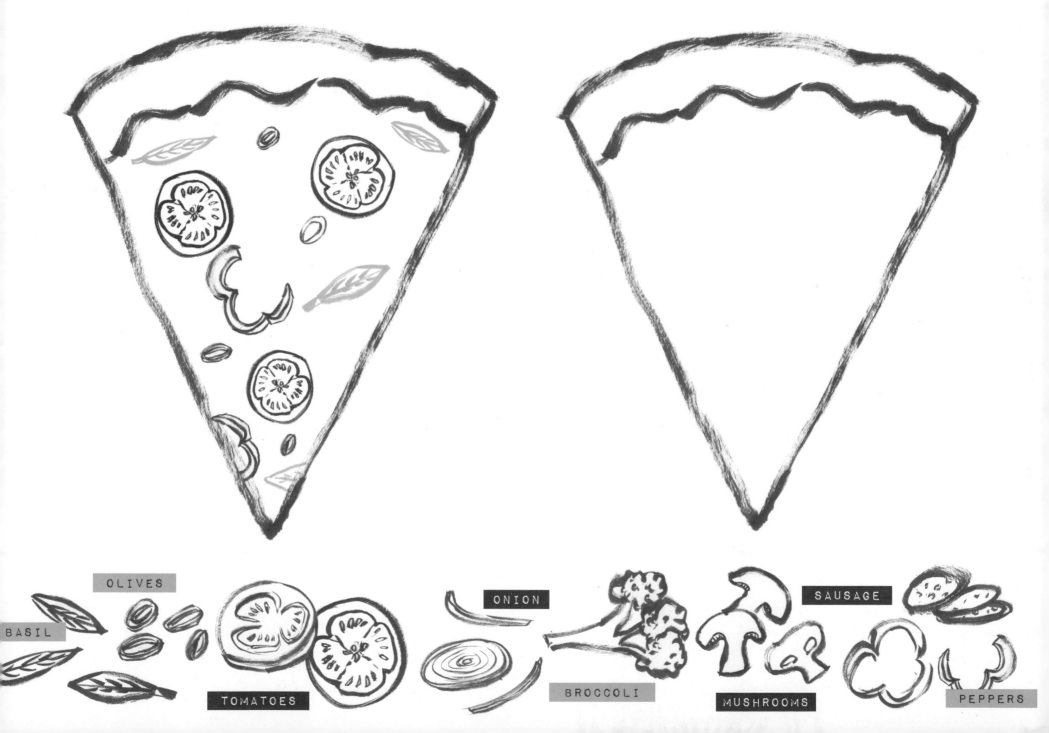

BASIL

OLIVES

TOMATOES

ONION

BROCCOLI

MUSHROOMS

SAUSAGE

PEPPERS

New Museum
of Contemporary Art

1902,
285 feet,
21 floors.

Flatiron
Building

MONKEY
BUSINESS

Draw the world's
most famous
gorilla, King Kong,
climbing on top of
the Empire State
Building.

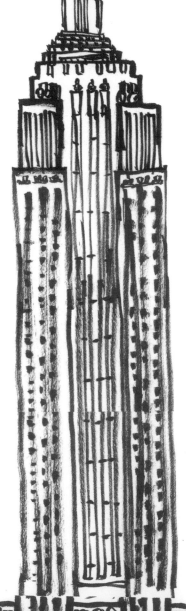

Empire
State
Building

1931,
1250 feet,
102 floors.

Have you noticed that all the skyscrapers have different tops?
At night they have light shows that color the city.

The
New York
Times
Building

2007,
1047 feet,
52 floors.

1930,
1047 feet,
77 floors.

Grand Central
Terminal

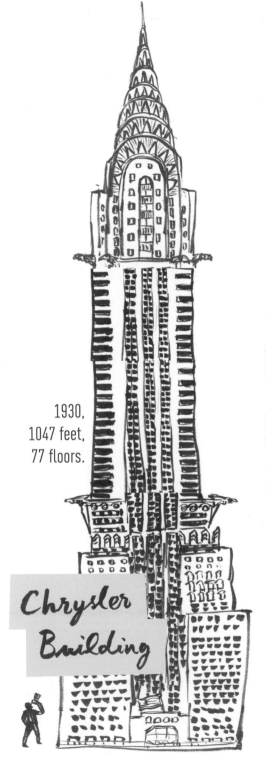
Chrysler
Building

HIGHER AND HIGHER

Finish these skyscrapers and make them as high as the sky!

Lightning rods are put
on top of skyscrapers
to protect them from
lightning. Fill the sky
with lightning and
add some rods to your
buildings to protect
them.

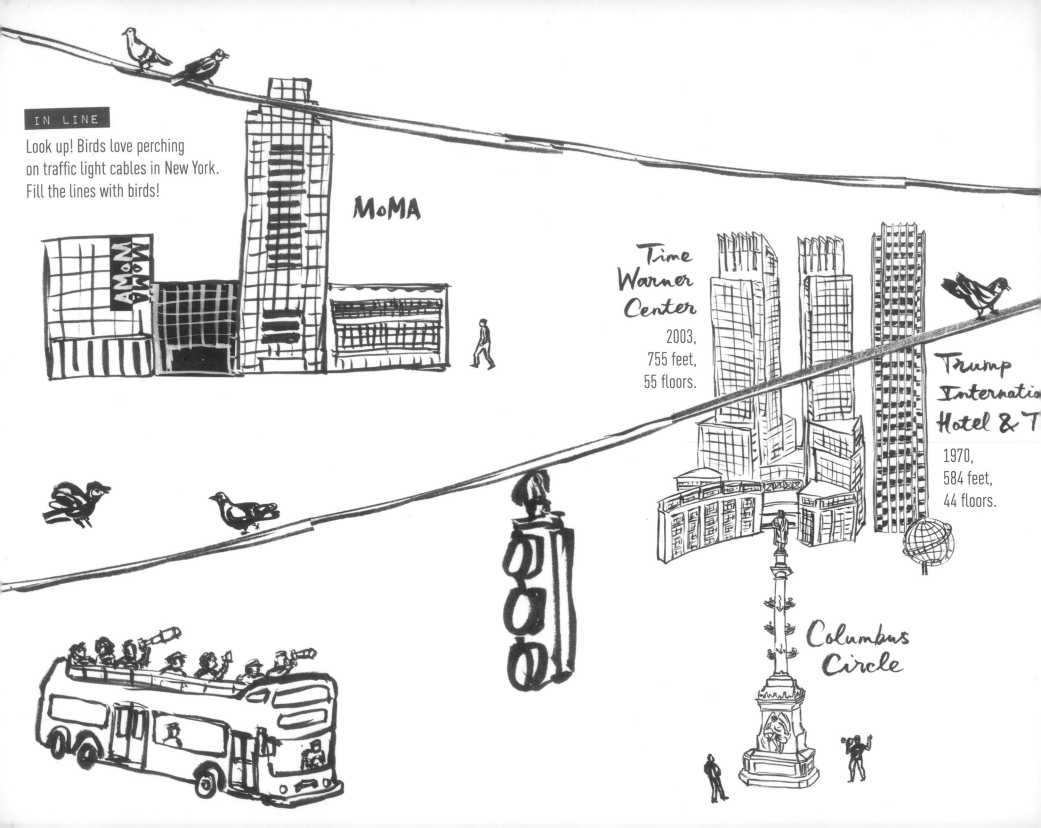

IN LINE

Look up! Birds love perching
on traffic light cables in New York.
Fill the lines with birds!

MoMA

Time
Warner
Center

2003,
755 feet,
55 floors.

Trump
Internatio
Hotel & T

1970,
584 feet,
44 floors.

Columbus
Circle

Plaza
Hotel

1907,
249 feet,
20 floors.

Summer

Sunbathing & boat trips

Spring
Ladybirds & picnics

Central Park

Experience Central Park all year round! Draw trees, flowers, and activities to show what you'd see in each season.

American Museum
of Natural History

Metropolitan
Museum of Art

HOWYADOOIN?

Museum Mile

Neue Galerie

Guggenheim

Jewish Museum

Cooper Hewitt

Winter

Snowmen & sledging

DOG ON A LEASH

How many dogs can you hold on a leash? Draw some other animals you'd like to take on a walk.

Fall

nimal tracks & colored leaves

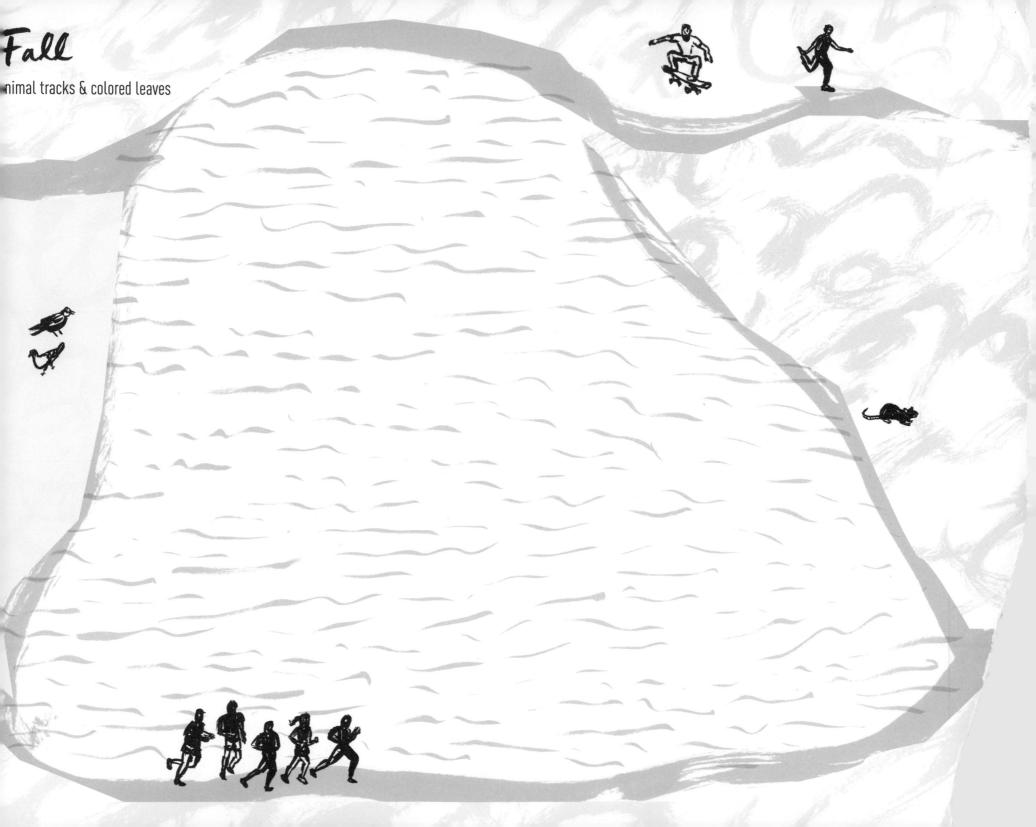

ve an art collection? Design your own museum on Museum Mile to show your treasures, objects, fossils, drawings, marbles, rocks ...

New York is one big movie set—hundreds of movies have been filmed on its streets. Step into the spotlight and draw yourself on set with your favorite actors.

TAKE: DAY: SCENE: MOVIE:

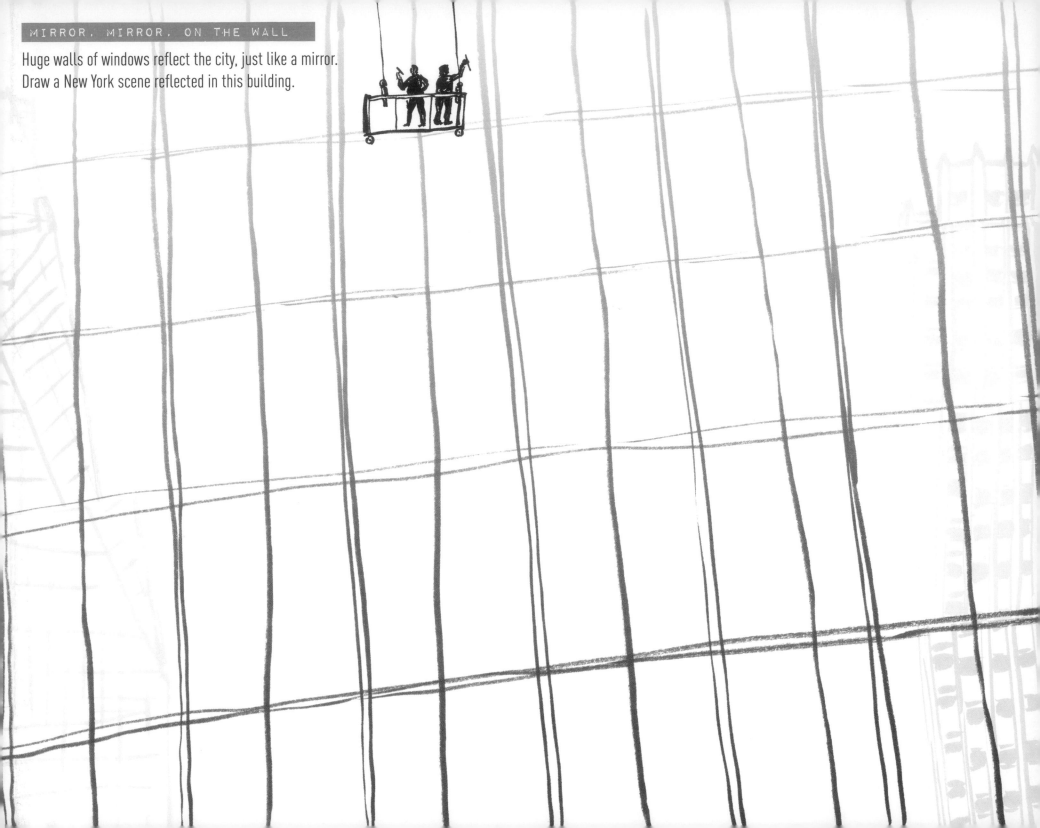

Huge walls of windows reflect the city, just like a mirror.
Draw a New York scene reflected in this building.

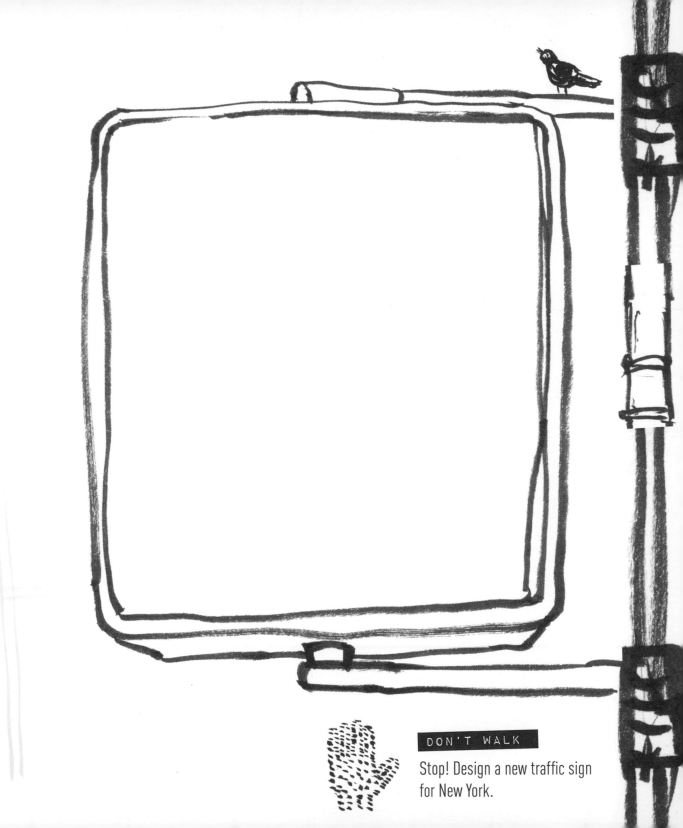

DON'T WALK

Stop! Design a new traffic sign for New York.

The New York Public Library

Rockefeller Center

Saint Patrick's Cathedral

COOL AS ICE

Draw as many skaters on the ice rink as possible!

Add huge balloons shaped like superheroes flying above the Thanksgiving Day Parade, or design your own cartoon character. Be a drawing hero!

NewYork Sightseeing

Hop on! What can you
see from the bus?
Draw your family and
friends on the top
deck, and don't forget
the view!

Create your own Times Square!
Invent your own companies and
design billboards for them to
fill the boxes.

On New Year's Eve people come to party on Times Square, and confetti falls from the sky at midnight. Fill the page with colorful confetti and people celebrating.

HI, FOLKS!

STREET FOOD

Food trucks in New York sell everything from bagels and pretzels to burgers and hot dogs. Fill this empty stand!

Color these doughuts and add your own! What toppings are you going to use?

The High Line

KEEN ON GREEN

Draw flowers, trees, butterflies, or bees.
Color this unused railroad green.

Hudson River

Whitney Museum of American Art

CAR PARK CHALLENGE

So many cars and not enough space! The NYC solution? Vertical parking.
Fit as many cars as you can in this vertical car park.

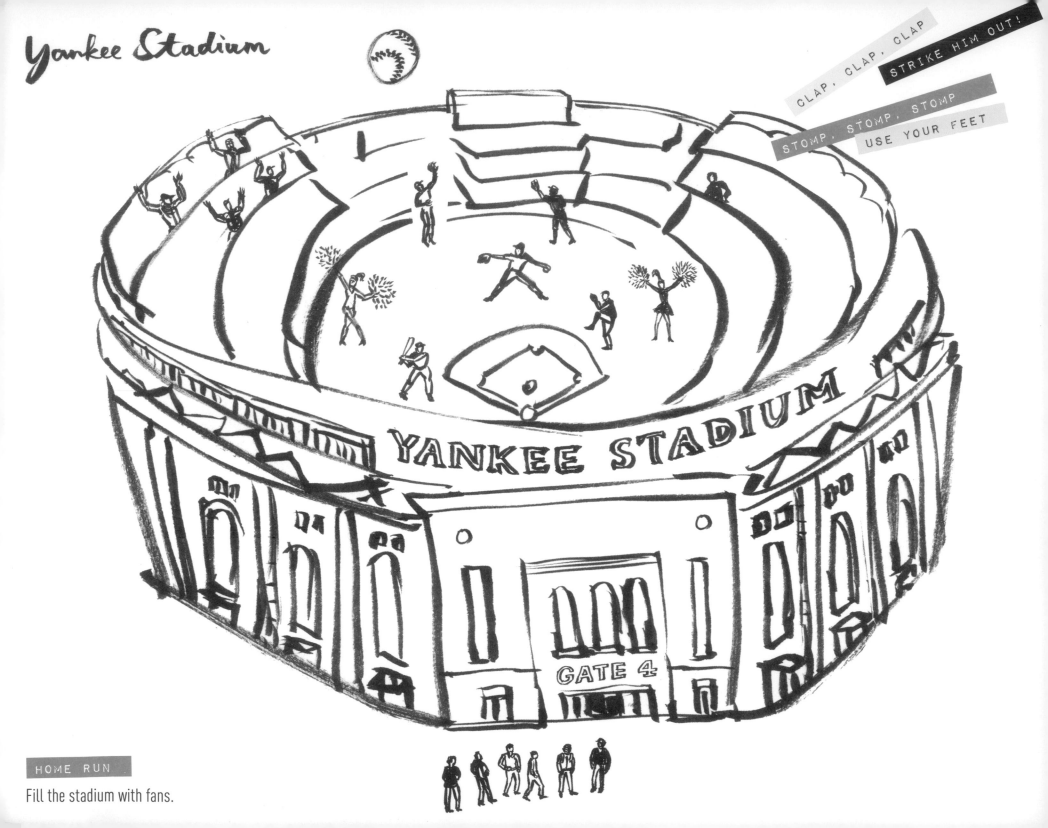

Yankee Stadium

CLAP, CLAP, CLAP
STRIKE HIM OUT!
STOMP, STOMP, STOMP
USE YOUR FEET

YANKEE STADIUM

GATE 4

HOME RUN

Fill the stadium with fans.

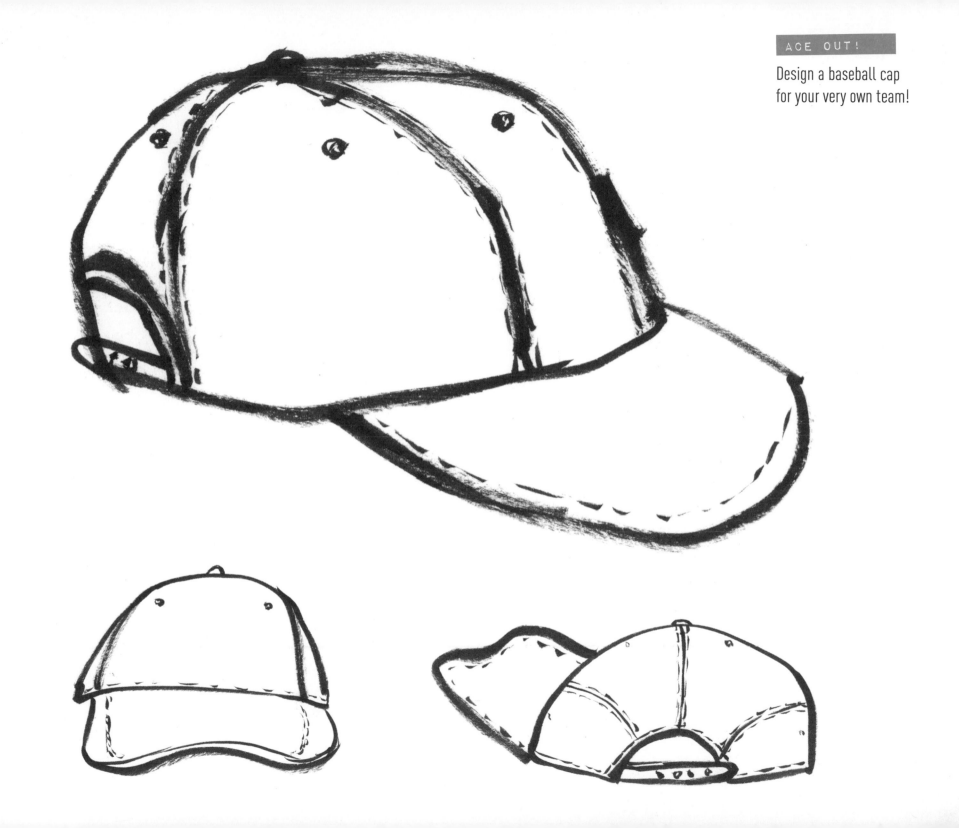

GRAFFITI
IN THE CITY

Originating in the New York City Subway,
graffiti art has an international influence.
Create your own graffiti here!

SEE YA!

What did you enjoy most in
My New York?